Lightning Shades

Also by Jessica Raschke and published by Ginninderra Press
Luscious Glass Cage
The Beguilings

Jessica Raschke

Lightning Shades

Acknowledgements

'dominion' appeared in *Bittersweet* at the 2010 Melbourne Writers Festival

'The Mystifed Set' was featured in the exhibition *Mystified* with photographic artist Maggie MacCathie-Nevile at VAC Gallery in Bendigo, November 2012

'Seeing in Layers' appeared in Issue Four of *Five Poetry Journal,* 2011

Dedicated to my little Raschke-Pettigrew family

Lightning Shades
ISBN 978 1 76109 057 8
Copyright © text Jessica Raschke 2021
Cover: Allison Colpoys

First published 2021 by
GINNINDERRA PRESS
PO Box 3461 Port Adelaide 5015
www.ginninderrapress.com.au

Contents

daydream drift	7
rust and rough	8
summertime blisters	9
unison, whirs automatic	10
calloused pride	11
love at home	12
the space with weight	13
wishing for a god	14
goodbye, my love	15
seeing in layers	16
the hauntings	17
soiled fingernails	19
natural history of awkward	20
tentative guest	21
where we go when forced	22
senseless seeing	23
The Mystified Set	24
the stillness eclipse	28
dominion	29
twilight wish	30

daydream drift

In all of this sticky
my eyes come to slow in a
daydream drift of afternoon:

the heat of the world
invites languor and doze.

And here I am, resenting a breeze,
and its insistent and tickly refresh.
'Don't wake him,' I whisper
'He's too beautiful right now.'

As his eyelids shimmer in quickened witnessing,
scouring the abstract laid in all that's being,
I know he's soaking in peculiar meanings…

And as his jawline relaxes in restful release,
I smile at those open lips, those deliverers of gentle heartness,
when they browse and tender-peck my waiting skin.

I thank the sticky air for bringing the slow,
for growing my lovingness for him:
a pensive form of relishing,
a daydream drift that's real.

rust and rough

As his rusted iron hair wires
spring from their cores,
his skin surface sparkles
with delight, gaggle giggle, and love

She sees: he took the slums into his heart
and: he loved its grit and scars.
He nested in its curves,
and found happiness in her roughs

Why claim the past is tense,
it's happening now, she can see,
she can feel the love coming
direct from his fiery heart lines

summertime blisters

in those summertimes
spent branding red to skin,
of mastering calculated crispiness,
of making a musical of blistered whims,
you lie down at night and softly bruise
as the moon shoots its glances at
your indiscretions.

you want the darkness to cocoon the foolishness
but lightness billows it through

and you see crumpled halos in every room
of your home

into the dusted air you speak
to raise questions of all the unfairs:

where is seclusion stored?
and where do blisters go?
where do glances direct themselves?
and why do summers spurn?

unison, whirs automatic

our faithful unison, whirs automatic:
our hands know routine like lungs bellow,
in time and attuned

I know you, don't I, don't you

expand the paper, brew the black drink,
sigh in words, smile in quarters…

our faithful unison, whirs automatic,
our legs set in distance, untouchable

our understanding is this knowingness,
and familiarity is the order of things

I know you, don't I, don't you

say again, your remembrance:
a day of red tones wooed in our acquaintance

and our own little cosmos grew
and
our shared eternity will reign beyond whirs

calloused pride

his hair crown of grey is threaded with veins of black
and it's crumpling in decomposition
as his gel product's efforts to turn it brilliant
are stripped of their poignancy:

a little but tenderly lame

wholesome years, are these?
without the padding of her stirring feet-steps he feels
the home's air is built from his sighs, not breaths,
always out, never in

and so it happens:
this home is now a house,
its unguarded weatherboards, weathered now

his shoulders arch in deference while
domed callouses grow strewn
across his crinkle-wrinkle skin:

a little but tenderly lame

aged and poorly, she went…
she went to the gone…

and he stays here with the gel product,
trying to preserve the decomposition.

love at home

she moved back into that house
and didn't imagine
the echoes would be so loud
for so long

she polished the walls, dusted the floors,
scraped the ceiling, wrestled the kitchen,
but the sounds of love pounded deeper

a teacup bearing flowers
gone pale from decades of washes
kisses her lips.

And that's it.

ceramic, porcelain and glass
could splinter and shred her face into strings
and swap the tears with blood

erase the waste:
the wasted time spent waiting
for love

the echoes, no one told her
the echoes, she could not see
were hauntings of the 'once fondness',
of the 'once love' that abounded
in the atmosphere:
more romantic –
more present –
than time wasted

the space with weight

In the centre of his red lounge room
he sits on a vinyl chair:
two-toned, a retro throne,
and he notices

her breaths remain here, while she's gone.

His imagination offered him more than this:
it performed scenes of pleasant tickle times,
and impassioned love months burnt to years,
it televised shows of tasty hug highlights,
with hearts matched perfect, little dears.

Instead blasé gestures called 'everyday'
and drawn voices titled 'comfortable'
sewed silent experiences to his skin:
ill-fitting and itchy and worn.

Then she enters the space with weight on her face
and his old hands drop to the floor…
no more will he hold it,
no more will he wait:

his imagination has let him down.

So he packs,
and says goodbye,
and takes the weight
from the space.

wishing for a god

he is sitting in a white box,
waiting for her to die

and in a droplet of salty water
there comes a tear,
a dewy portion of silver-truth,
with fear-admission packed in tight:
erasable and wipeable…
and there he goes: *swipe*

    – from the back of a beady hand
    – a dream of love and life gets crushed

a bigger man would permit her release,
to ease the aches that stall his heart,
but his invisible toil of wanting love is preferred:
the only time he's wished for a god.

goodbye, my love

as if your slight squeeze of my hand
is enough to say goodbye…

remember, I always resented your half-smiled hellos
as if my loving presence
was enough to keep you suspicious

give me salty sobs and grunt-growl howls
give me tidal waves of anguish and laments
and give me blood-blistered eyes, ready
to disintegrate from all those hard tears

don't give way, my love, don't…
or is this just nature's very truth?
But it can always be turned false, you said
with your invincible muscleman words

resist, my love, resist
know that our bodies will no more feel
their fiery skins together

they will no more know
their fuse-bound 'just us' warmth

there was always love, my love,
and it will stay here, ready for your return

(you will, my love, you will)

rage, my love, rage
when you squeeze your final goodbye

seeing in layers

Every landscape is layered –

    a rhyme under that weeping willow
    an epic beneath that bended blade of grass
    and another ode will sprout from that rosebush next spring

It invites you –

    brush the earth with your struck eyes
    as if sight were yours
    for the first time

Every landscape is layered –

    not by rock
    not by sediment
    nor dirt

    but by lives
    and their histories
    and universal sounds uttered
    like never before

    a fading baby's last cough
    a lion's first step on its paw
    the padded buzz of an insect's last fly of its wings

All are here, among the layers.

the hauntings

eloquence is a furious hurricane,
it whirls and consumes and turns dizzy
all of the known elements

and when it wanes I watch the water
turn to waves in sunset heat…
and so the hurricane goes, it goes in a snap,
and its echoes just slide away…

but they haunt my system until
I'm spread and crippled and still,
beset by a self-conscious mind

I'm left alone, sometimes, with the ghosts of this,
of the eloquence that once occupied;
they jeer and they groan as they hand me in bones
this utterly frugal offer:
a steel-grey shroud of cold-frigid air

apparently

it's some comfort against
the impending reheating,
the slow build up of hurricane wild

I wait…

the waves reverse the water,
the sun rises like a shadow,
and I can see it, the prospect:

of being silk smooth again
of being a slick social delight
and of being another cruisy-witty raconteur
who wraps them all, whatever audience there is,
in a hurricane of searing hot air

soiled fingernails

the soil is blackened and fragile, like death,
and between her rustic fingers it crumbles
until she reshapes it into rows of sunken cups
into which seeds will be sorted

the grit is her favoured feeling,
it scours her palms and turns her fingernails
into crescents of worm-soaked filth,
and the air is rank with dirt scent

if only earth energy could be taken
to all places:

to posh parties sodden with dwindling discussion,
and rampant with the crass loudness of sozzled chatter
about no things (in particular)

to mid-morning brunches on glistening café strips
scattered with well-groomed mothers from the right side
of all things

the soil carries comfort like wisdoms
only encountered by accident when digging

the earth energy, she knows, is helping her grow,
and she can bury the posh and the right

natural history of awkward

the natural history of awkward
of what I almost always feel –
am I sliced by red tremor cells/
am I rolled together by inadequate quells/

(This is the most sophisticated part of me.)
(The reluctance, the shyness, and all of the uneasiness…)

the natural history of awkward
of what I almost always feel –
I am made of these swinging limbs/
I am encased into a self/

(This is the best part of me, the one that I do not let be.)
(The kindness, the loving, the wiseness, the knowing, the showing, the loveness.)

the nights are gold-generous gestures,
bringing rest and murmur-talk,
and the innocent breathing that just goes on and on,
is most unaffected, is most authentic.

the truth best hums in all of this
like smouldering acquiescence:
it sweeps aside all of them,
those hesitant unsteady confusions.

It trickles into silence.
    What I almost always feel –

It shifts into unnatural.
    What I almost always feel –

tentative guest

my being is a tentative guest
in this blemished womanly form:
curves, scars and softness
are markings bare for seeing: *it's me*

but this is shell and this is husk,
so I crouch and scrape the deeps
in hunt for the one in possession of it:
that's it, *my actual identity*

so…*in the meantime*

my head is lobbed into the vagues,
and my thoughts are elongations of yours…

to be unpoetical, to be anything 'un'
to be chameleon, body and mind…
perhaps I am this, or I am to be
someone where 'defined' needs remind

where we go when forced

a sweeping scent of possibles
rides my ambivalent face…

it pinches the air and
flicks all of its life-giving force…
inside the scent, embedded,
are all of our mysteries

ancient breaths are there everyday
whispering, 'Existence is an ordinary word,'
yet in the place of those possibles
rest answers we cannot record

stay silent, stay quiet,
listen to what's within

is this life and its wonder,
is this life and its pause,
and is this the life we go to
when we are forced?

senseless seeing

blackness: where the most is seen
in the surrender of
sensorial testimony

no shadows push the walls
no illumination flourishes in its vast

blackness: where the most is released
in the wildlife of
senseless seeing

The Mystified Set

insistent illusions

the light dissolves as I
blanket my day-sight
with one long-lasting blink

and

upon the closure of reality
a suffusion of new territories
collapse into my consciousness

the no-sense nonsense,
a carousel of

>   *image*
>   face
>   *image*
>   mask
>   *image*
>   darkness
>   *image*
>   lightness

I weave a flight into unsightly spaces,
bear witness to their being

as if for the first time
as if for the only time

in this reckless landscape
cocooned in my decaying matter
where my unlived lives suggest themselves
in persistent, insistent, illusions

coloured moments

when the colours speak
the language goes hollow,
and my voice lacks presence:
it languishes in the spectrum
of reds and blues and greens

overwhelmed, I watch,
but there is only so much I can see
and make sense of…
and there is only so much I can be sure
comes from me…

flashes of colour crack into the white light,
and they illuminate many moments:
they are only sharp times
caught in instants
that will be forgotten (or re-remembered) when I wake

something of my self

there is no compass
pointing to spot-fires of reason:
instead it is legless drift and thoughtless daze,
and sometimes falling,
and sometimes flying.

I can see past faces,
younger than ever registered,
imbued with symbols, mouthing messages
that I can't hear or comprehend:
so I try, with my hands, to touch

my fingertips have numbed
insensitive and senseless
and I am guessing and I am hoping
to regain at least something
of my self

the mystified

the dew-morning light awakens me
and I haul the dreamy dark
into the day; I feel haunted by shady echoes…

absorbed into my being are
suggestions of words and images
stolen from the sensational worlds traversed
throughout the mess of night

I hold the weight of alternate lives,
I see the world through a hazy lens,
and, I wonder, *What world is this now?*
Is this the one meant for me?
Does my night mind take me to elsewheres,
better suited to my destinies?

loaded, my heavy soul-cells swim
like drunks in day reality;
they hold much of the night…
until it comes, *the forgetting,*
the immersion in
wakefulness,
and the absence of
the mystified

the stillness eclipse

Stillness is an eclipse of nature,
a quiet call that asks its forces
to lie low, to morph into hollow,
and to cry without any suggestion
of itself.

In the stillness eclipse,
in its unnerving quietude,
a death never ceases
to move.

And the hours were heavy with
no things, you see
and the seconds dropped in hangs of slow.

A heaving heart may pause in its pounding,
steady breaths may halt in their passage,
and death may appear still,
as it wants to.

Yet the decompose, it lives,
and the journey to the elsewhere,
just goes
       and goes
              and goes.

dominion

how many shades and subtleties decay
from inattention?

and how can intangibles grow true
without loving and fierce intention?

these elusive energies belie our truths
and our reaching for freedom.

once air-light beings, are we just bellows turned to dust,
the consequence of constant reject?

yes, the dust dispersed may be all there is:

it's time I reach mine,
my dominion in the shades,
my home in the subtleties.

twilight wish

my only wish/
for my twilight/
is to hum no regrets…

and

for the twilight/
to set at/
ever-lightning speed…

and

for my being/
to return/
in a flash…

www.ingramcontent.com/pod-product-compliance
Lightning Source LLC
Chambersburg PA
CBHW062207100526
44589CB00014B/2003